MW00356047

THIS BLUEPRINT BELONGS TO

....

....

....

....

~ DEDICATION ~

*To the patients, families, and caregivers who
touched my heart and motivated me to write.*

*To my family who are beyond a dream come true
for a mother and grandmother.*

*To Hank, my husband, my soulmate, my heartbeat.
You fill my heart with love and joy every day.*

Create a Unique Legacy

THE BLUEPRINT TO

AGE YOUR WAY

Gather your information.
Document your wishes.
Avoid the unthinkable.

DEBBIE PEARSON, RN

FAMILY NIGHT PRESS

AUSTIN•TEXAS

www.FamilyNightPress.com

© 2017 Debbie Pearson. All rights reserved. No part of this book may be reproduced in any form or by any electronic or mechanical means, including information storage and retrieval systems, without permission in writing from the publisher, except by a reviewer who may quote brief passages in a review.

ISBN 978-0-9978533-1-5
Library of Congress Control Number: 2016912340

Publishing manager: Janica Smith, *www.PublishingSmith.com*
Copyeditor: Lisa Canfield, *www.copycoachlisa.com*
Book design by Monica Thomas for TLC Graphics, *www.TLCGraphics.com*

Limit of Liability/Disclaimer of Warranty: While the publisher and author have used their best efforts in preparing this book, they make no representations or warranties with respect to the accuracy or completeness of the contents of this book and specifically disclaim any implied warranties of merchantability or fitness for a particular purpose. No warranty may be created or extended by sales representatives or written sales materials. The advice and strategies contained herein may not be suitable for your situation. You should consult with a professional where appropriate. Neither the publisher nor author shall be liable for any loss of profit or any other commercial damages, including but not limited to special, incidental, consequential, or other damages.

Printed in the United States of America

TABLE of CONTENTS

The documents enclosed speak for you if you can't speak for yourself.
This is a repository of what's needed for care and management of you.

BLUEPRINT FORMS

Additional lines are available on the back of each form
when more room is needed or for updates.

Congratulations!

Congratulations on launching the *Age Your Way Program*—your path to *Avoid the Unthinkable.*

You are embarking on a preemptive strike against the possibility of losing control over your life due to aging or illness. The structured format provides a way to record vital information and document wishes whether you're looking ahead to your own future or scrambling to assist an elderly relative in crisis.

With this book as your guide, your personal plan will leave no question about unique wishes for both living and dying; more than that, the Blueprint will include legal, medical, and financial information that will be essential to executing your strategy. After all, the aging years can last decades; shouldn't they be lived the way you want to live them?

Conversations are invaluable for thinking out loud and helping to crystallize beliefs. But the spoken word is subject to interpretation and memory. Details of discussions often evaporate, especially when stress enters the picture. Even those of us who have already designated an advocate to manage and support our choices must keep in mind that life offers no guarantees.

This completed Blueprint enables your advocate to step in and assist, equipped with an unambiguous foundation of individualized information. It also allows another to help if your named advocate becomes unable to assist as you expected.

When shared, your Blueprint will provide a gift to your family, saving them from the agony of choosing for you while they debate over who can better read your mind. Documentation is crucial, since aging or injury could hinder your speech or ability to direct decision making on what only you know for sure: the things that matter most to you. If that time comes, what's in your Blueprint will serve as your voice.

Thoughts before You Start Work

How challenging could it be to enter information into a book? Why is any form of guidance needed? I'll briefly share three different patient stories I encountered while planning for others and then we will move forward.

Allen was a tough guy, ex-felon who had served hard time. He became my patient after a prison explosion burned sixty percent of his body and required partial amputations of all four of his limbs. The fact that we had successfully worked through many challenges together over more than a decade gave me a false sense of calm when we embarked on his aging plan.

I thought I knew him well and anticipated no problems. Boy, was I wrong! Tears flowed intermittently throughout the planning process followed by a period of depression. For a lifetime, Allen had avoided facing fears, wishes, and his own mortality. He'd simply assumed his existing support system would stay rock-solid for the remainder of his life. "What ifs" never entered his consciousness. From Allen's eruption of unexpected emotions, I learned to approach every planning session with a healthy degree of trepidation.

On the other hand, Grace was as excited as a young woman on prom night. For weeks, she gathered documents in advance and prepared for our initial meeting. She already functioned in the dual role of caregiver for her frail elderly husband and for her adult disabled daughter. Now was her turn. It was time to focus on her life, to evaluate plans, and to document her own "what ifs." Grace's relief was visceral as we planned for the three individuals who were the responsibility of one.

Carl was the cautious type, the planner, surely the poster child for the *Age Your Way Program*. Not quite. As a retired professor, he had all the intellect required to gather documents and actively guide necessary decisions. However, as a methodical worker with a slowing of cognitive function, each step took significant time to think through and prepare. I learned how to carefully watch for signs of mental and emotional fatigue so Carl was not pushed to do more than he could stand during any one session. He taught me how to be patient at a new level.

Heighten Your Sensitivity Meter

Implementing this program demands an abundance of respect and sensitivity. Although some of you will execute your own Blueprint, a large number of individuals will require an advocate for all or part of the planning. If you are the advocate, then please treat this as a position of trust, confidentiality, and neutrality, especially as you gather personal documents. Continue to think how you would feel if the roles were reversed and someone else had the task of digging into all the corners of your life. How uncomfortable would that be?

And keep in mind, your role is not to guide or judge decisions. Rather, it is to extract and record someone else's decisions to ensure their Blueprint is just that: *theirs*. An accurate accounting of *their* wishes. *Their* unique plan. We all have our own perspective on finances, health, and how we want our lives to be lived. All advocates are tasked with the *neutral* role of documenting for others, not guiding responses. Once completed, the plan serves as a gold mine of information, exclusive to that individual.

Many people approach the planning process at the stage when the majority of their active lives are in the past. As for the present, some remain happily occupied, but for others, longstanding networks are not necessarily reliable: friends or siblings may have died, some relationships may not have stood the test of time, and others may be developing stress fractures. Meanwhile, finances may be falling short and health isn't guaranteed. A few cases may reveal problems without hope of resolution and a foundation of disorder. Your kindness and support are the gifts you have to offer. Use these gifts wisely and learn as you go.

The process can be exhausting, so don't push, and don't rush. Always allow the person you are assisting to set the pace. Whatever works for them is the right pace. If you are launching your own plan, then apply the same patience and kindness to yourself. It took years to amass the layers of your life, the texture that makes you unique. Documenting and gathering everything takes time.

Identify Your Stage for Planning

A key ingredient for figuring out where to go from here is accurately defining *here*. What is your stage, here and now? Time for honesty. Glance through the chapters that follow. This will help you understand the complexity and level of detail required to complete your Blueprint. If you no longer have the energy or ability to gather and document everything that is required, then ask for help. No family member will reject your request for assistance as this will simplify their lives tremendously down the road. The three stages are listed below.

- Stage One is where *you* are in control of planning. People who are in Stage One are sharp-minded and can follow a structured format. They retain abundant physical and mental energy, and they'll need every bit of it to independently create their own Blueprint, which accurately reflects them.

- Stage Two is where the individual requires *assistance*. These individuals may have been reluctant to plan, in denial, or simply unaware. They can express their wishes and provide information. However, they no longer have the ability or energy to keep the planning process moving forward in an organized manner. They need help to extract wishes and locate valuable information. The person assisting them—maybe that's you—serves as hunter-gatherer for documentation. Done right, the completed plan is still an accurate Blueprint of the individual's information and wishes.

- Stage Three is where someone else does the best they can to *handle another's crisis*. Ability to state wishes may be limited or completely absent. Gathering data is tortuous and frequently erroneous. Vital pieces of the puzzle are often missing. The plan may not reflect who that person is or what they want. Personal control is lost. Even so, the Blueprint provides a valuable structure for knowing what information needs to be gathered.

Frequently Asked Questions

Where to start?

Your Blueprint is divided into chapters but can be worked in any order that makes sense. It's all important, but some concerns are more urgent than others. Start with those. A scan of chapter headings will help you quickly identify problem sections. For instance, if health is precarious and no legal documents are in place, then look to medical and legal chapters as priorities. If finances are in total disarray, then that may be the logical first step.

How long will this take?

People can concentrate on this work in small chunks, usually one to four hours at a single session. It is remarkable how quickly the time elapses. Usually, two hours is most comfortable. Two hours today, two hours tomorrow, next week, next month, a sustained effort. For my own plan, I needed months to assemble the extensive unrelated and overlapping elements. I was surprised at how long it took but will be forever grateful that I got it done, rather than leaving it to someone else at a time when I couldn't participate.

Who holds on to the book during the working process?

Typically you (or the advocate) retains physical control of the Blueprint while the work evolves. This tactic protects the process, keeps it on track and helps avoid the sense of being overwhelmed by looking at all the unfinished chapters. It's vital to maintain the book in a secure and confidential manner until completion when there will be a determination of where the Blueprint and gathered documents will be secured.

Is a "to do" list a good idea when helping someone else gather their information?

While meetings are ongoing, it's wise to maintain duplicate to-do lists for both the individual and the advocate. But with so many working parts, a lengthy list can be too much. It's preferable to build in a few minutes at the end of each session to create a new list, and keep it short. The work is hard, but a careful advocate can help avoid discouragement while keeping the process on track.

Can we really talk about money?

What a touchy subject! All their lives, some folks cling to rules of social etiquette, including this: Nice people don't discuss money. Naturally, some individuals worry about revealing their finances to their advocate and even to family members. However, full financial disclosure is not the intent of the Blueprint. The goal is to know where assets can be found when needed, not the dollar value of each asset. Account co-signers can be designated for emergency purposes only, without access to full financial information in advance of the need.

Is this a one-time process?

Not necessarily. Things change, so the plan should accommodate revision through the years. I advise an annual personal meeting with the advocate and/or family to review updates and convey any new information.

Blueprint Logistics:
Gathering & Documenting

Start either at chapter one or with another chapter that screams out as the most glaring need. While working through the chapters, you will both complete forms in the Blueprint as well as gather additional information to form a comprehensive plan. Keep collected documents in a single place, corresponding to the chapters in the Blueprint. The papers can be organized in hanging files, an accordion file, or in folders. To be the most helpful to others, label files or sections of your accordion file to correspond with the headings of each chapter of the Blueprint. Finishing one section at a time maintains order.

You may be tempted to use one book for a married couple. This is how I started in working with patients in their homes. It seemed logical to me. But, what I found was that two people in one Blueprint resulted in confusion. Each had different insurance cards, individual legal documents, and unique wishes. Through trial and error, I learned that the cleanest method was to have a Blueprint and documents file for each individual. Then, the final reason is that couples die at different times. Having a Blueprint and set of files for each individual will preserve their unique plan intact.

How do I manage information
that changes over time?

Some of the items you document will not change like date of birth, military ID number, social security number, names of children, etc. Other information will likely evolve. For variable items, you have two options. Either document in pencil and use erasers. Or, you can write in ink, mark through outdated items, and utilize the available space for edits. Many forms have adequate room to incorporate modifications. Should space be inadequate, lined space is on the back of each form for additions.

What Happens When You're Finished?

Meet with the responsible party or family to share the information in your Blueprint. It is a precious compilation to benefit both the individual and family. Bringing the individual and designated parties together yearly for updates can enhance relationships and sustain the Blueprint's efficacy.

Complete the *Distribution Document* that follows the *Table of Contents*. This form identifies who has copies of what part of the plan.

Decide where to keep the Blueprint and files, some place secure but easily retrievable in a time of need. This may be tricky. You don't want private personal and financial data to fall into the wrong hands. It's for designated individuals, period. For that reason, the entire plan should be locked in an area accessible only to your informed inner circle. But for them, twenty-four-hour availability is paramount, especially for critical medical and legal information. In case of emergency, ready access enables immediate response.

DISTRIBUTION DOCUMENTS FOR:

Name _____

*This distribution list is executed **after** the Blueprint is completed*

AFTER the blueprint is completed, this form lists who has copies of what items. Your name goes in one column & other names are listed in columns to the right. Place an ✗ in columns to indicate who has documents from each chapter.

CHAPTER ITEMS	Your name	Names of people who have been given copies of documents			
Legal/ Other Documents					
Medical					
Phone Numbers					
ID Cards/ Credit Cards/Mail					
Banking/ Safe Deposit Box					
Assets					
Income					
Obligations					
Insurance/ Potential Benefits					
Log-ins/Passwords/ PINS/Keys					
Funeral/Burial/ Special Requests					
Guide to Decision Making/ Treatment Options					
Care and Placement Alternatives					
Other					

Legal/Other Documents

It always strikes me odd that most people have a will in place long before any other legal documents. The will addresses what takes place after death. But what about all the years while you're still alive? Those are the years in which your plan will be felt and experienced by you. Maintaining control while alive is what the *Blueprint to Age Your Way* is about.

If you do nothing else in planning, take the deep dive into your legal paperwork! Some of you will want to close this book right now at the prospect of such a dive. But wait! With guidance and grit, you too can swim. You can tiptoe into the water by checking online where you'll find some of the necessary documents, but read the fine print. States have varying requirements, so make sure the documents you download comply with your state's particular laws. Even better, meet with an attorney and execute all your documents simultaneously. Over the years, I have seen disasters averted by well-written and customized legal documents. True, an attorney costs money. But it's an investment, and you—and those who'll survive you or support you in the case of disability—are worth it.

Copies of all legal and other documents should be together. The ideal set-up is to keep original documents in a safety deposit box or safe, with copies in your *Blueprint to Age Your Way* filing system. You may not need all the following documents, but those underlined are absolutely necessary.

- **<u>Medical Power of Attorney</u>** (manage medical)
- **<u>Durable Power of Attorney</u>** (manage finances)
- **<u>Directive to Physician</u>** (document end-of-life wishes)
- **<u>HIPAA Release of Information</u>**—Health Insurance Portability & Accountability Act (establishes who can receive your medical information)
- **<u>Will and Designation of Executor</u>** (how your estate will be distributed after your death and who will carry out your wishes)
- **Guardianship designation in the event of incapacity** (who you would want to be your guardian if you are incapacitated)
- **Disposition of Remains** (where you want your remains placed if you are cremated)
- **Statement if you wish to be an organ donor** (download form from Internet)
- **Important:** When designating legal responsibility, don't risk the chance of your documents becoming obsolete. If your named responsible party dies or is unable to perform the job, then someone else must be listed as an alternate. It is best to designate one to two younger alternates who would remain available for many years to come.

Other important documents may have been in the same place for years. You know where, but someone else might need to search for weeks to find these items. By including them in your filing system, you simply make it easier for someone to assist you when that time comes.

- Birth certificate
- Marriage certificate
- Children's birth certificates
- Adoption papers
- Pre-nuptial agreement
- Trust agreements
- Partnership agreements
- Tax returns
- Any other legal or contractual documents

LOCATION OF LEGAL DOCUMENTS

Information on where to find documents and who is the responsible party.
Clearly describe where the originals can be found so someone else can locate them.
Place copies in your file. Blank spaces have been added to allow for other documents.

Document	Location of original document	Responsible party or parties
Medical POA (manage medical)		Named parties (in order)
Durable POA (manage money)		Named parties (in order)
HIPAA (who can obtain medical information)		Named parties
Directive to Physician (end-of- life instructions)		
Will or Trust (after death)		Executor of your will or trustee
Guardianship Designation (if needed)		Named parties (in order)

(page 1 of 2)

Document	Location of original document	Responsible party or parties
Disposition of Remains (if being cremated)		
Organ Donor Authorization		
Other		

LOCATION OF OTHER DOCUMENTS

Identify location of originals. Place copies in your files.

Document	Where originals are located
Your birth certificate	
Your children's birth certificates	
Children's adoption papers	
Marriage certificate	
Divorce papers	
Pre-nuptial agreement	
Trust agreement	
Partnership agreement	
Income tax returns	
Other	
Other	
Other	
Other	
Other	
Other	

....

....

....

....

....

....

....

....

....

....

....

....

....

....

....

....

....

CHAPTER 2

Medical

This chapter requires medical expertise: it is the only section that is best completed with outside help. Involve someone who has a clinical background—a doctor, nurse practitioner, physician's assistant, geriatrician, or registered nurse. For you to make informed decisions, you need to understand your alternatives. In the past, people became ill, aged, and died of natural causes. With the medical technology available today, this is no longer the case. We have options to intervene, changing or delaying nature's cycle. That's why you must document your wishes point-by-point. Before you get sick, it's easier to get inside your own head and determine your individual philosophy concerning life, death, and illness. Legal documents are broad; your plan is best followed by means of written specifics.

The medical helper you choose should have the broadest possible experience, both hospital inpatient and outpatient knowledge. All decisions have life implications to be considered, details to be explained. Don't select an option without understanding how it would impact your day-to-day existence. There are no right or wrong choices, merely what best defines the way you choose to live.

To find your medical helper, a good place to start is with your primary care physician, his or her nurse, a home-health nurse, or medical case manager who takes this role seriously. Along with making sure the person has suitable medical experience, ask the question—do they *really listen* to *you*? Will they spend enough time to ensure you completely understand and document your preference for care? Networking in your community is another excellent approach. Or, you can search web-based sources for geriatric care managers or case managers.

A comprehensive medical plan should include these written documents (forms included):

- My Medical Demographics
- Photocopy of medical insurance, prescription cards, photo ID
- Medical Planning Worksheet
- Setting of priorities
- List of your favorites, what you truly enjoy
- List of fears
- Concessions you are willing to make when needed
- Preference for CPR

My Medical Demographics

As medical care becomes more complex and fragmented, we find ourselves repeating the same information over and over again. Although medical providers all have some form of electronic medical record, no single platform communicates among all providers.

The solution to this problem is available through *My Medical Demographics*. This format puts you in control to collate all your medical information in one location that you own, update, and photocopy to use as needed. It condenses critical data about you into a single document: Medical conditions, medications, emergency contacts, doctors, and more. Not only is the structure efficient, it actually improves medical care. But to be effective, the data must be current, concise, and comprehensive.

When time is of the essence, *My Medical Demographics* can speak for you and quickly inform emergency services or other medical personnel of everything they need to know at a glance. Then they can focus on treating your current problem. Hundreds of times I've seen this condensed form work in a way that expedites needed care. It is a must for everyone.

In my life as a nurse case manager, we called 911 many times for patient emergencies. The minute EMS arrived and we handed them the condensed medical information, the reaction was always the same: Visible relief. After a brief moment for review, they could go straight to work, managing the emergency. No wasted time. All of us can read much faster than we can listen to information, and emergency workers are no different. That's why you need a readily available, organized document.

You may require assistance to complete your *My Medical Demographics* form. If so, use your medical helper to get you started. When finished, it's imperative to make copies and keep extras readily available for emergency workers or unplanned medical care.

IMPORTANT

- ❧ Update your *My Medical Demographics* as medications, conditions, and doctors change.
- ❧ Keep copies available for emergencies and unplanned medical care.
- ❧ Take copies to all doctor appointments.
- ❧ When changes occur, update your document, **shred old copies** and make new ones.

MY MEDICAL DEMOGRAPHICS

Download a copy of this form at AgeYourWay.com

Name (on medical records & health insurance)	
Date of Birth	Social Security #
Cell Phone	Home Phone
Address	
Drug Allergies	
Pharmacy (name, address, phone #)	
Hospital Preference	
Height	Diet (list restrictions)
Weight	
Special Instructions for EMS—note if full CPR, Out-of-Hospital-Do-Not-Resuscitate, or on Hospice Care	
Home Health Agency, Hospice Agency, or Case Management Company—enter name and phone number	

(page 1 of 6)

Name _____ Date of Birth _____

Medical History—Diagnoses that your doctors list in their records. Include body systems of heart, head (neuro), gastroenterology, urology, lung, orthopedic, endocrine, psychiatric, cancer, skin, pain, eyes, ears.

Surgical History—Include surgery and date (approximate if exact date not known).

Name _____ Date of Birth _____

Medication name and dose. Prescription, over-the-counter, and meds used only as needed.	Times taken per day	Prescribing Doctor	Put ✗ for time medication is taken			
			A.M.	Lunch	Supper	Bed
EXAMPLE Lipitor 20 mg	1	Herb Smith				✗

(page 3 of 6)

Download a copy of this form at AgeYourWay.com

Name _____ Date of Birth _____

EMERGENCY & OTHER PERSONAL PRIORITY CONTACTS *List Medical Power of Attorney first*		
Name	Relationship	Phone #s

DOCTORS		
Name	Specialty	Phone # / Address
	Primary Care	
	Dentist	

Name _____ Date of Birth _____

MEDICAL INSURANCE		
Insurance Name	Policy / ID #	Phone # / Other identifying information
1st		
2nd		
Rx		
Dental		
Other funding option for medical care		
Other health insurance		

LAST DATE OF IMMUNIZATIONS / ROUTINE DIAGNOSTIC TESTING		
Flu Shot	Pneumonia Vaccine	Shingles Vaccine
Tetanus	Colonoscopy	Mammogram
Bone Density		

(page 5 of 6)

Name _____ Date of Birth _____

LIVING ENVIRONMENT — ASSISTANCE NEEDED
Living environment (home, assisted living, etc.):
Assistance needed with what activities of daily living:
Caregivers who assist:
Medical equipment, supplies currently used:
Any other information needed for care:

Photocopy medical insurance and identification cards. IMPORTANT: Place copies of medical cards, prescription cards, and photo identification along with your *My Medical Demographics*. Copy front and back of all cards. Include cards that identify your pacemaker or other medically implanted device.

Medical Planning Worksheet

The *Medical Planning Worksheet* addresses decisions you might encounter, either down the road with natural aging or from a sudden change in your health status. It lists both short-term and long-term medical interventions aimed at sustaining life. I'll repeat myself at this point because this is so important to understand and get right.

Many years ago, when modern medical interventions were not available, lives ended from natural causes. Now we have the option of prolonging life by a variety of manmade means. While you are healthy and mentally sharp, it's the ideal time to think through what decisions you would want if illness or injury rendered you unable to think or unable to communicate your wishes. The *Medical Planning Worksheet* is NOT a legally binding document. Instead, it serves as a reference for your responsible party. Even if you're unable to talk, this document reflects your stated wishes and can serve as an invaluable guide. If your wishes change at any time, simply re-do the document.

Several states have initiated similar forms. Some of the current names are **POLST** (Physician Orders for Life-Sustaining Treatment) and **MOLST** (Medical Orders for Life-Sustaining Treatment). These state-approved, doctor-signed forms are meant to take effect if your condition becomes such that your physician would not be surprised by your death in the next year. At the writing of this book, the states that have these forms available are Oregon, West Virginia, Wisconsin, California, New York, New Jersey, Indiana, and Nevada.

In contrast, the *Medical Planning Worksheet* is designed to be executed at any time of your life so that your wishes regarding artificial life support become a part of your advance planning documents. In my many years of nursing, I've worked with a multitude of families who wished they had some guidance from a loved one who lost the ability to provide any direction. The worksheet is to be used only in the event that you are unable to communicate wishes and your responsible party or surrogate decision-maker requires guidance from an earlier time when you were able to document wishes.

Instructions for Completing Your Medical Planning Worksheet

- Locate your medical helper as described earlier. Make sure the helper understands the worksheet's purpose: **It is to be safeguarded for use in the event you lose ability to communicate wishes and your surrogate decision maker requires guidance from an earlier time when you were able to document wishes.**

- Review the worksheet in advance. Make a note of questions or unclear sections.

- Schedule an appointment allowing adequate time for questions to be asked and answered. It should take less than thirty minutes to complete this document.

- The form can be finalized with just the individual and the medical helper.

- Some individual patients wish to have their surrogate decision maker (medical power of attorney) also present. I find this helpful so that the surrogate is aware of the choices in advance.

- Keep in mind that the answer to each scenario is the **patient's decision**. There should be no attempt to influence the choices by either the surrogate or the medical helper. These are personal wishes by an individual for his or her own planning.

- Treatment options to consider are interventions against catastrophic injury or illness, such as traumatic brain injury or stroke. If you lose the ability to communicate, family members will be asked what treatments they want applied. Your wishes in advance can be very helpful. However, you must understand this is **not a legally binding document**. It is merely a guide to help your family or surrogate decision maker arrive at choices that are consistent with who you are and what you want.

- There are two columns to the right. The first column is to reflect your choices when there is clear and convincing evidence that you will never be able to regain mental awareness or independent functioning. You would be in a persistent vegetative state, forever dependent on life support and care by others.

- The second column presents a situation where the prognosis is poor but uncertain. There is a small but unclear chance you might regain some level of awareness or live with a limited degree of independence one day. This scenario is not optimistic but allows for some unknown outcome.

- By answering questions ahead of the need, you'll lighten the already significant emotional burden others may carry as a result of your medical crisis. Family is relieved of difficult decisions and can simply apply choices you made in advance.

- On the top of the form, enter the patient's name (the one they use for medical records), date of birth, and the worksheet's completion date.

- Answers in the boxes are to be documented as yes or no.

- Signature lines are at the bottom for the patient, medical helper, and others who witnessed the discussion. The medical helper is to also indicate their credential (MD, RN, etc.)

- If your primary care physician is not the person helping you complete the form, it's a good idea to provide him or her with a copy, as a part of your official medical record.

- Your responsible parties need to know where this completed form is or have copies.

MEDICAL PLANNING WORKSHEET / COMMUNICATING PERSONAL WISHES

Name _____ Date of Birth _____ Date _____

This is <u>NOT</u> a legal document but a guide for considering and recording personal wishes.
When unable to direct your care, this becomes a refresher for your surrogate decision maker.

If overwhelming illness or brain damage prevents high-level thinking or communication, these are my wishes.		
Treatment Options to Consider	**No possible chance of awareness or living independently** (answer yes or no)	**Small but uncertain chance of awareness or living independently** (answer yes or no)
Cardiopulmonary resuscitation. Use of pressure on the chest, drugs, electric shocks, and artificial breathing to revive me if I die.		
External non-invasive positive pressure airway breathing (no intubation—like CPAP) short-term.		
Ventilator <u>short-term</u>. Breathing through a tube inserted through the mouth into my windpipe.		
Ventilator <u>long-term</u>. Surgical opening placed in my neck (trachea) to attach a breathing machine.		
Artificial feeding <u>short-term</u> through a tube from nose into the stomach (1–2 weeks maximum).		
Artificial feeding <u>long-term</u>. A permanent tube inserted in my stomach through my abdomen used to provide liquid nutrition from outside my body.		
Kidney dialysis. Cleaning the blood by machine. Blood is removed & cleaned 3 times a week in a dialysis center (3–4 hours each day).		
Invasive diagnostic tests. For example, examining the stomach through a tube or viewing heart circulation by injecting dye (angiogram).		
Pacemaker—surgical implantation of a device that maintains heartbeat at a prescribed rate.		
Transfusion of blood or blood components.		
Intravenous antibiotics to fight infection.		
Major surgery—examples: removing part of the intestine, hip repair after fracture, etc.		
Comfort care to treat pain, anxiety, discomfort.		
AFTER DEATH: Organ donation?		

Signatures of those involved in the discussion / relationship:

_____ _____
Patient Documenting Wishes   Medical Helper (and credential)

_____ _____
Witness (if present but not required)   Witness (if present but not required)

Priorities, Favorites, and Fears

The priorities, favorites, and fears documents are a marvelous resource for others involved in your life. I can't even begin to count the number of times I wanted this information on my patients, but their time to communicate was in the past. Imagine taking a wild guess at what brings joy to someone else. How hollow that feels! And, by contrast, how gratifying to know for sure. Some patients say they're terrified of dying alone. Others worry that they won't be able to look out a window or have hot coffee in the morning. These nuggets of knowledge are powerful. If you're the patient, you can rest assured that your intimate worries will be more likely taken into account when they are documented. And if you're the patient's family, you'll be better able to enhance your loved one's final chapter.

Setting of Priorities

All of us have priorities in our lives, unique to our experiences, values, and relationships. Because preferences may change as circumstances change, three columns provide space to update your priority list over time. Blank lines provide space for you to specify other priorities.

List these in order of number one, two, or three with number one being the most important to you. It's possible to have multiple items with the same rank. Write "no" if the item is not important to you at all.

Favorites and Fears

Regarding favorites and fears, this is your opportunity to go on record in helping others to know you better. Do you always like your toast dry, your water with ice, your music classical? Document those things here. One day you may not be able to communicate your wishes clearly. Take advantage of that opportunity now as there may be circumstances where the person closest to you will not be able to communicate on your behalf. These planning documents are designed for anyone to utilize in setting up your environment the way you want.

SETTING PRIORITIES FOR:

Name _____

Number your priorities (1, 2, 3, or no. #1 is the highest priority)
This is a way to document what matters most on a specific date. Make revisions under a
new column date any time your situation changes. Use blank spaces to specify additional priorities.

Date choices made	Date choices made	Date choices made	Priority
			Remain together with your spouse
			Stay in your own house
			Choose where you move from your house
			Have a private room in a facility (short- or long-term)
			Continue smoking
			Continue drinking alcohol (includes wine and beer)
			Remain together with your pet
			Continue driving
			Maintain electronic communication
			Maintain control over your finances
			Remain alive in all circumstances
			Receive comfort care only (end-of-life/terminal)
			Be given last rites prior to death
			Leave a financial legacy to your heirs even if quality of your care suffers for this priority

Signature _____

FAVORITES

Describe what would be your perfect day. How would you use your time?

_____

_____

_____

_____

_____

_____

_____

_____

FEARS

List fears you'd like others to know if you are unable to make them known.

_____

_____

_____

_____

_____

_____

_____

_____

_____

Signature _____

FAVORITE THINGS

Foods, music, books, movies, TV programs, activities
(This helps others to support what you most enjoy if you are unable to communicate)

Foods	
Music	
Books	
Movies	
TV Programs	
Activities	
Other favorites	

Signature _____

Concessions I Agree to Make

❧ "You can't always get what you want," the song lyric goes, which is why your plan must include concessions. This is a medical *plan*, not a medical pipe-dream, so it has to be practical. How many of us have tried to talk a parent out of driving because of safety concerns? We involve doctors, we arrange painful family interventions, we try everything in our power. Sometimes, our best efforts fall short.

❧ That's why the plan includes a list of concessions you'd be willing to make when needed, such as driving, moving out of your house, etc. When topics being discussed appear years or decades away, it's easy to be logical and understand the rationale behind the needed changes. When the years diminish our insight and increase our entrenchment, it helps to look back at concessions made at an earlier time. Your own signed agreement carries weight.

❧ Enter your name and signature on the form and document below what concessions you'd be willing to make when various situations arise. Feel free to be as specific as you wish to adequately describe what those concessions would look like. Whereas not all will occur, most of us will need to make one or two concessions for safety or financial reasons.

CONCESSIONS I AGREE TO MAKE

Name _____

When you are told it is no longer safe for you to drive (by family and/or doctor)

_____

_____

_____

When you can no longer remain alone in your house safely

_____

_____

_____

When you and your spouse require different levels of supportive care

_____

_____

_____

When you are alone & family support is in another city

_____

_____

_____

When you can no longer keep your pets

_____

_____

_____

Signature _____ Date _____

Preference for CPR (Cardio-Pulmonary-Resuscitation)

Preference for CPR finishes out your plan's medical section. This is not as clear-cut as it appears. People who have thoughtfully considered and documented their preferences in legal papers are often lulled into a false sense of security. If an ambulance shows up at your door, do you think your carefully worded legal documents will protect your end-of-life wishes? Ninety percent of my patients and families think so. But they're wrong.

Your "Directive to Physician" is a valuable legal document, helpful in making decisions with all facts considered. But its value flies out the window once EMS (emergency medical services) is involved. For these situations, you need a different form, the DNR (do not resuscitate) state-approved directive. This directs EMS to *not* perform CPR, if that is your wish, allowing a natural death instead.

In an emergency, EMS will never stop to read legal documents. When a patient has no heartbeat and isn't breathing, every second counts. Paramedics go straight to CPR. That's their job. They'll stop for just one thing: If someone hands them the out-of-hospital DNR form as they enter the house. Whatever your legal documents say about your wishes makes no difference to EMS.

When the DNR instruction is in place and presented, then EMS workers **will** treat all other emergency conditions and transport you to the hospital when indicated. The only thing they will not do is to perform CPR if you have already died.

Therefore, if you or your loved one wishes to *allow a natural death* and not be revived if death occurs in the home, it's essential to complete the EMS document that clarifies this wish in advance. Search the internet for the Out-of-Hospital DNR form for your specific state. You may want to meet with your physician and discuss your wishes, then complete the document. Most states require a physician's signature for the form to be valid. Your doctor also knows your medical conditions and can offer advice.

It's important to note, this document is specifically designed to be effective when *out of the hospital setting*. This can be in the home, nursing home, assisted living, ambulance, or anywhere apart from the hospital. Once you pass through the hospital doors, the Out-of-Hospital DNR form is no longer effective. However, your advocate may find it useful as evidence to argue your wishes, should you become nonverbal or incapacitated while in the hospital. The more extensive, specific, and accessible your advance documentation, the greater the chance your wishes will prevail.

If you can speak for yourself when admitted to the hospital, you can and should direct your "code status." In hospital lingo, "coding" refers to the moment when a patient experiences cardiac or respiratory arrest. "Code status" is the hospital's own term. Unless clarified otherwise, everyone is a "full code" when entering the hospital, which means CPR will be performed. Should this not be your wish or not be the wish of your loved one, a talk with the attending hospital doctor will be needed to initiate a DNR order for that hospital stay.

Phone Numbers

Collect phone numbers and other contact information for family, personal, and business contacts (copy cards where available). Include family, attorney, accountant, financial advisor, insurance broker, and other important numbers. It is also important to include phone numbers for services such as housekeeper, yard service, pest control, home repairs, etc. Should something happen where you can no longer manage scheduling of services, it's advantageous for someone else to know which individuals and firms you trust to do the work.

The grid that follows can be utilized to document numbers by hand or copies of contacts can be obtained by any means that is comprehensive.

Hint: review address books, Rolodex, computer contacts, cards that are posted, refrigerator magnet information, papers in drawers. All the categories listed have value.

- Family & Friends
- Business Contacts
- Service Providers
- Other

FAMILY / FRIEND

Circle if the person is family or friend.

Name	Category	Phone Numbers / Email Address if you correspond in writing.
	Family Friend	
	Family Friend	
	Family Friend	
	Family Friend	
	Family Friend	
	Family Friend	
	Family Friend	
	Family Friend	
	Family Friend	

(page 1 of 2)

Name	Category	Phone Numbers / Email Address if you correspond in writing.
	Family Friend	
	Family Friend	
	Family Friend	
	Family Friend	
	Family Friend	
	Family Friend	
	Family Friend	
	Family Friend	
	Family Friend	
	Family Friend	

(page 2 of 2)

BUSINESS / PROFESSIONAL CONTACTS

Add to list as needed. (Doctors should be in the medical chapter.)

Name	Category	Phone Numbers / Email
	Attorney	
	Financial Investments	
	Financial Advisor	
	Accountant	
	Insurance Broker	
	Banker or Trust Officer	
	Church or Minister	
	Club or Organization	

(page 1 of 2)

Name	Category	Phone Numbers / Email
		_____
		_____
		_____
		_____
		_____
		_____
		_____
		_____
		_____
		_____

(page 2 of 2)

SERVICE PROVIDERS

Add to list as needed.

Name	Category	Phone Numbers / Email
	Home Repairs	
	House Cleaning	
	Lawn Care	
	Accountant	
	Home Security System	
	Pest Control	
	Plumbing	
	Electrical	
	Heating/AC Repairs	

(page 1 of 3)

Name	Category	Phone Numbers / Email
	Barber or Beauty Shop	
	Phone Service	
	Cable & Internet	
	Home Medical Provider	
	Equipment Supplier	
	Provider of Medical Disposable Supplies	
	Care Giver	
	Home Health Care Service	
	Case Manager	

(page 2 of 3)

Name	Category	Phone Numbers / Email

(page 3 of 3)

OTHERS

Name	Category	Phone Numbers / Email

(page 1 of 2)

Name	Category	Phone Numbers / Email

(page 2 of 2)

CHAPTER 4

ID Cards/Credit Cards/Mail

This documentation provides information to others who may be assisting you. In addition, including copies is a tremendous help to you if your cards are lost or stolen.

Instructions: Copy front & back of all listed plus write date next to copied card.

- Medical Cards
  - Medicare card
  - Medicare supplement
  - Prescription card
  - Commercial Health Insurance
  - Any other medical cards (vision, dental, etc.)
- Any other cards you have that might be needed by another
  - Pacemaker ID
  - Any other medical devices or implants
  - Cards that you carry in your wallet that are important
- Driver's license or state ID card. If license is out of date, that's okay. The card is valuable as a photo ID.
- Passport

- Credit Cards
  - Next to card copy, list others who have credit cards on this account.
  - If you are the only one on credit cards, do you need to add someone else to enable purchases for you in the event of emergency?
- Military discharge document (DD214)
  - If no document available, list:

    Branch of military

    _____

    Enlistment date

    _____

    Discharge date

    _____

    Military ID number

    _____

    Rank at discharge

    _____

MAILBOX ID

Location of Box	Box Number	Key Location

SOCIAL SECURITY ID

For you, your spouse, children (very helpful for legal & estate situations).

Legal Name	Social Security Number	Relationship

CARD INFORMATION

If you are unable to make copies of cards, document card information below.
Medical, insurance, driver's license, passport, credit cards, military.

(page 1 of 3)

If you are unable to make copies of cards, document card information below.

If you are unable to make copies of cards, document card information below.

(page 3 of 3)

Banking

Financial concerns can be a source of consternation, especially if resources are slim, deep, or chaotic. Many people are sensitive about sharing personal financial information. Don't worry; you don't have to reveal specific dollar amounts. What your family needs to know is the location of resources and where to obtain information should you become incapacitated. Don't saddle them with such tasks as tracking down bank accounts, investments, and real estate. Provide information on your income stream and your recurring obligations. Be particularly clear about direct deposits and automatic withdrawals.

Your family must know what account receives Social Security and other recurring deposits, such as pension and IRA disbursements. In an attempt to simplify matters, some families move forward quickly to consolidate multiple bank accounts. This can be a drastic mistake. **Any account that receives direct deposits must remain open to retain the benefit.** Accounts can be consolidated, but only after the direct deposit benefit has successfully transferred to another bank account. If the account that receives your Social Security check is closed, then the government automatically assumes death and deposits will immediately cease. With cancellation of Social Security payments, your Medicare health insurance also ends. For that reason, a very strong warning to family members is below.

CAUTION: To Family & Responsible Party

Don't lose benefits by closing or consolidating bank accounts! You must clarify which accounts receive direct deposits and automatic payments for Social Security, pension, IRA, etc. Do *NOT* close any account where these payments are deposited. If the Social Security direct-deposit account is closed, there will be an automatic assumption that the individual has died and deposits will immediately cease. Along with deposits ending, Medicare and any insurance coverage associated with Medicare will stop. Providing evidence that the individual is still alive and getting benefits re-started can take months!!! While waiting, the cost of medical care will need to be paid out-of-pocket.

In addition, you must not close accounts before clarifying whether money is deducted regularly (whether monthly, quarterly or annually) from the account for automatic payments. When accounts are closed, vital benefits like medical insurance and long-term care insurance can be lost forever.

Bank Accounts

List Checking, Money Market, Savings Accounts on the following pages.

Even better, place copies of statements with your documents to reflect all information.

You should designate a trusted individual as a co-signer on at least one account with enough cash flow to take over bill payment in the event of an emergency. This can be a family member, trusted friend, or a company (fiduciary) that manages bill payment. When ill or incapacitated, you will certainly want someone to step in and manage your financial responsibilities. The best way to ensure this is by providing the information and adding one person to your account.

BANK ACCOUNT INFORMATION

Account type (circle one):   Checking   Savings   Money Market   Other

Account # _____

(Attach voided check or statement of account if possible)

Bank Routing # _____ Bank _____

Exact name on account _____

Who signs on the account _____

_____

Does there need to be a signer added in the event of emergency (recommended for at least the primary operational account). If so, who is that?

_____

In general, what account is used for _____

_____

_____

What items are direct deposited to this account and at what frequency

_____

_____

What items are directly drafted from this account and at what frequency

_____

_____

_____

_____

(page 1 of 6)

Account type (circle one):   Checking   Savings   Money Market   Other

Account # _____

(Attach voided check or statement of account if possible)

Bank Routing # _____ Bank _____

Exact name on account _____

Who signs on the account _____

_____

Does there need to be a signer added in the event of emergency (recommended for at least the primary operational account). If so, who is that?

_____

In general, what account is used for _____

_____

_____

What items are direct deposited to this account and at what frequency

_____

_____

What items are directly drafted from this account and at what frequency

_____

_____

_____

_____

_____

_____

(page 2 of 6)

Account type (circle one):   Checking   Savings   Money Market   Other

Account # _____

(Attach voided check or statement of account if possible)

Bank Routing # _____   Bank _____

Exact name on account _____

Who signs on the account _____

_____

Does there need to be a signer added in the event of emergency (recommended for at least the primary operational account). If so, who is that?

_____

In general, what account is used for _____

_____

_____

What items are direct deposited to this account and at what frequency

_____

_____

What items are directly drafted from this account and at what frequency

_____

_____

_____

_____

_____

_____

_____

(page 3 of 6)

Account type (circle one):   **Checking**   **Savings**   **Money Market**   **Other**

Account # _____

(Attach voided check or statement of account if possible)

Bank Routing # _____ Bank _____

Exact name on account _____

Who signs on the account _____

_____

Does there need to be a signer added in the event of emergency (recommended for at least the primary operational account). If so, who is that?

_____

In general, what account is used for _____

_____

_____

What items are direct deposited to this account and at what frequency

_____

_____

What items are directly drafted from this account and at what frequency

_____

_____

_____

_____

_____

_____

(page 4 of 6)

Account type (circle one):   Checking   Savings   Money Market   Other

Account # _____

(Attach voided check or statement of account if possible)

Bank Routing #_____   Bank _____

Exact name on account _____

Who signs on the account _____

_____

Does there need to be a signer added in the event of emergency (recommended for at least the primary operational account). If so, who is that?

_____

In general, what account is used for _____

_____

_____

What items are direct deposited to this account and at what frequency

_____

_____

What items are directly drafted from this account and at what frequency

_____

_____

_____

_____

_____

_____

(page 5 of 6)

Account type (circle one):   **Checking**   **Savings**   **Money Market**   **Other**

Account # _____

(Attach voided check or statement of account if possible)

Bank Routing # _____ Bank _____

Exact name on account _____

Who signs on the account _____

_____

Does there need to be a signer added in the event of emergency (recommended for at least the primary operational account). If so, who is that?

_____

In general, what account is used for _____

_____

_____

What items are direct deposited to this account and at what frequency

_____

_____

What items are directly drafted from this account and at what frequency

_____

_____

_____

_____

_____

_____

_____

(page 6 of 6)

SAFETY DEPOSIT BOX

Bank Name_____

Address _____

_____

Box # _____

Who is authorized to access the box _____

_____

Who has keys?_____

_____

Location of your key _____

_____

Should an additional authorized user be added and, if so, who is that?

_____

_____

_____

Any special items or legal documents kept in the box

_____

_____

_____

_____

_____

_____

(page 1 of 2)

Bank Name _____

Address _____

_____

Box # _____

Who is authorized to access the box _____

_____

Who has keys? _____

_____

Location of your key _____

_____

Should an additional authorized user be added and, if so, who is that?

_____

_____

_____

Any special items or legal documents kept in the box

_____

_____

_____

_____

_____

_____

_____

(page 2 of 2)

Assets That You Own

Through the years, we accumulate things that we own. Some are fairly new acquisitions, some quite old or maybe even inherited from previous generations. This chapter will help you document everything of economic value that you own. Below is a list of assets I have helped my patients research and list. However, the list may not be all-inclusive so add whatever assets will make your list complete.

- Investment Accounts
  - Certificates of Deposit / Annuities
  - Stocks / Bonds / Commodities
  - Oil & Mineral Rights
  - Other investments
- Business holdings
  - Joint ventures
  - Percentage ownership
  - Inventory
  - Equipment
  - Trademarks, copyrights, patents, etc.
  - Accounts receivable or loans

- Real Estate
  - Residence
  - Rental property
  - Vacation home
  - Time share
  - Farm or agricultural holdings
  - Other property
- Vehicles (list make, model, mileage as of this date)
  - Cars
  - Boat
  - Recreational vehicle
  - Other type of vehicle
- Other items of value or insured
  - Art
  - Jewelry
  - Coins
  - Other collections

INVESTMENT ACCOUNTS

Certificates of Deposit • Annuities • Stocks
Bonds • Commodities • Oil & Mineral Rights • Other Investments

Description of Asset	Where Located	Contact Person's Information

BUSINESS HOLDINGS

Joint Ventures • Percentage Ownership • Inventory • Equipment
Trademarks, Copyrights, Patents, etc. • Accounts Receivables or Loans

Description of Asset	Where Located	Contact Person's Information

REAL ESTATE

Residence • Rental Property • Vacation Home • Time Share
Farm or Agricultural Holdings • Other Property

Description of Asset	Where Located	Contact Person's Information

VEHICLES

Vehicles • Cars, Boat, Recreational Vehicle, Other Type of Vehicle
(List make, model, mileage at this date)

Description of Vehicle	Make, model, mileage, other information. Where located.

OTHER ITEMS OF VALUE OR INSURED

Art, jewelry, coins, other collections

Description of Asset	Where Located	Other Information

CHAPTER 7

Income

Your advocate or assistant will need to know what comes in and goes out of your accounts. Some funds flow in monthly, others quarterly or annually. Keep this part of your Blueprint handy to add or delete as changes occur. It is critical to document what accounts receive these income streams so no accounts are inadvertently closed, therefore ending the benefit.

It is very helpful to add photocopies/paperwork of all these income sources to your files. These copies often supply additional information required for your helper.

Another excellent means of identifying all sources of income is to look at tax returns. All income that comes in to you should show up if you review the last two years of tax returns. This can help jog your memory.

- Social Security
- Retirement
- Military / VA
- IRAs
- Annuity
- Investment Dividends
- Oil & Gas
- Rental Income
- Business Income
- Other Income

SOURCES OF INCOME

Make copies of all documents for details.

What	$ Amount	Frequency	What bank account?	Whose name is on the payment
Social Security				
Retirement				
Military / VA				
IRAs				
Annuity				
Investment Dividends				
Oil & Gas				
Rental Property				
Business Income				
Other Income				
Other Income				

(page 1 of 2)

Make copies of all documents for details.

What	$ Amount	Frequency	What bank account?	Whose name is on the payment

(page 2 of 2)

Obligations

As important as income is to your plan, it's also necessary to think about outflow. This section is designed to assure your obligations are met on a consistent and timely basis. Of special importance are automatic deductions from your bank accounts for health insurance, utilities, rent or mortgage, and a whole host of items that keep your world running smoothly.

For items automatically paid by credit card, you will also need to provide that information in this section.

It is very helpful to add photocopies/paperwork of all these obligations to your files. These supporting documents often supply additional information required for your helper.

If paper bills are sent to the house, then listing of expenses is less critical. Where people get in trouble is missing information on items that are automatically paid, which results in lack of awareness.

Add to and edit items as they change.

- Housing Cost (rent, mortgage, utilities, etc.)
- Community Fee
- Vehicle
- Insurance
- Credit Cards
- Taxes (quarterly estimates, property, other)
- Loan
- Membership
- Insurance (health, other)
- Other Obligations

OBLIGATIONS

Make copies of all documents for details.

What	$ Amount	Frequency	How Paid?	Name on the Bill?
Housing (rent, mortgage, etc.)				
Community Fee				
Vehicle				
Vehicle				
Credit Card				
Credit Card				
Taxes (quarterly)				
Taxes (property)				
Taxes (other)				
Loan				
Memberships				
Health Insurances				
Other Insurances				
Other Insurances				

(page 1 of 2)

List all household and recurring bills that are paid directly by
bank draft or credit card and other obligations.

What	$ Amount	Frequency	How Paid?	Name on the Bill?

(page 2 of 2)

Insurance/Potential Benefits

This section can serve to direct others to potential benefits. When you have gone to the effort to maintain policies or benefit packages, you certainly want the people designated by you to have access to all forms of assistance that may enhance your care or situation.

Whenever possible, place the benefit plan information in your files.

The list below is to jog your memory of what you might have in place.

- Long-Term Care Insurance
- Disability Insurance
- Life Insurance
- Household Insurance (homeowner or renter)
- Accident Insurance
- Auto Insurance
- Umbrella Policy Insurance
- Civil Service / Veteran's / Employer Insurance
- Any Other Insurance

INSURANCE INFORMATION

Insurance (copy cards / policies as available) / Potential Benefits

Type of Insurance Company	$ Value	Who does it cover?	Broker Name & Contact Information
Long-Term Care			
For Long-Term Care Insurance, make a copy of the policy limits / dollar amounts and copy the entire policy for explanation, limitations, and contact information. Place copy in files.			
Disability			
Life			
Household Homeowner's Renter's			
Accident			
Auto			
Umbrella			

(page 1 of 2)

Insurance (copy cards/policies as available)/Potential Benefits

Type of Insurance Company	$ Value	Who does it cover?	Broker Name & Contact Information
Civil Service			
Veteran's			
Employer			
Other			
Other			

(page 2 of 2)

CHAPTER 10

Log-ins/Passwords/PINs/Keys

It is a continual surprise how much of our lives can be halted without the proper log-in or password. This is a challenge for most of us to keep up with on a daily basis. Imagine someone else being put in the position of helping you without any of this information.

LOCKED ITEMS & AREAS

For any of these locked areas, provide information below to access and open.

Item	Location of Item	Key Location or Combination
Vault/Safe		
Locked File		
Padlock		
Storage Unit		
Other		
Other		

LOG-INS / PASSWORDS

It's preferable to have log-ins and passwords listed in a secure software application that can be passed along to a trusted family member or responsible party.

Website	Log-in / Password	Other Information / Name on Account

(page 1 of 4)

Website	Log-in / Password	Other Information / Name on Account

(page 2 of 4)

Website	Log-in / Password	Other Information / Name on Account

(page 3 of 4)

Website	Log-in / Password	Other Information / Name on Account

(page 4 of 4)

CHAPTER 11

Funeral, Burial, Wishes

This subject can be touchy. However, it is a reality for every one of us. Typically, dealing with funeral arrangements comes at a time of high emotion. For that reason, many funerals are based on the feelings of a grieving family, rather than on the individual wishes of the person who has died.

Documenting your wishes in advance is a gift. It costs nothing to meet with a mortuary and pre-arrange your funeral, so everyone should take this step. Even better, do both the pre-arranging and pre-payment. That is the ultimate gift! At the time of death, bank accounts can be frozen for a period of time. Why not relieve both the emotional and financial burden on those you leave behind?

It's typical for people to not anticipate the importance and volume of demographic information required for funeral arrangements. Most of us would not have all of another person's needed data. Therefore, forms follow for you to complete so that you will have everything documented in advance for your loved ones. This part of the Blueprint includes:

- ᪥ Fears regarding aging and death
- ᪥ Funeral and burial wishes
- ᪥ Obituary or items to include in your obituary
- ᪥ Specific bequests to others
- ᪥ Funeral information to gather in advance

FEARS REGARDING AGING & DEATH

Name _____

Help others to understand your fears so they can mitigate these effects on your behalf.

_____

_____

_____

_____

_____

_____

_____

_____

_____

_____

_____

_____

_____

_____

_____

_____

_____

_____

_____

_____

FUNERAL & BURIAL WISHES

Name _____

Funeral wishes—traditional, cremation, donation of body	
Funeral home—name, address, phone number	
Location for memorial service	
Service specifics—open or closed casket, religious considerations, etc.	
Cemetery preference, location, phone number. If plot owned, document plot number and place copy of information in files.	
Disposition of cremains if cremation is the choice. Where do you want your ashes?	

(page 1 of 2)

Clergy preference, church, and contact information	
Music preference	
Preference for scriptures, other prayers, speakers	
Casket bearers (names & contact information)	
Preference for flowers or other memorial ideas	
Other wishes	
Is pre-arrangement done? Is the funeral pre-paid? Place copy of pre-paid contract in files.	

(page 2 of 2)

OBITUARY

Name _____

Some people are very comfortable providing input for their obituary while others are not. There is no right or wrong. What helps is to take a moment and communicate your wishes to others.

Do you want a detailed obituary or a simple death announcement in the local paper?	
Where do you want your obituary to be seen? Any specific publications?	
Family members or special people you want mentioned in your obituary.	
Are there particular aspects of your personal life or career you would like mentioned in your obituary? If so, what?	
If you have written your own obituary, indicate so here and place it in your files.	

SPECIFIC BEQUESTS

If you believe any of your family heirlooms and sentimental objects have special significance to someone you care about, list below. It is a good idea to talk with the individuals about these matters. You may find someone has a special attachment to a certain item that none of the others care much about anyway. This list is independent of your legal will. It covers personal items, not necessarily objects of great monetary value.

Name _____

Description of Item	Who Gets It Name & Contact Information	Location of Item

(page 1 of 2)

Description of Item	Who Gets It Name & Contact Information	Location of Item

(page 2 of 2)

FUNERAL INFORMATION TO GATHER IN ADVANCE

Full legal name (first, middle, last) _____

Address _____

City/State/Zip Code _____

Phone _____

Email _____

Sex _____ Race _____ Date of Birth _____

Father's name (first, middle, last) _____

Birthplace of father _____

Mother's name (first, middle, last) _____

Birthplace of mother _____

Your birthplace (city/state) _____ Citizenship _____

Education level completed/institution(s) _____

_____

_____

Social Security # _____ Veteran (yes/no) _____

Branch of military _____

Rank at discharge _____ Service number _____

Enlistment date/place _____

Discharge date/place _____

Location of military discharge papers _____

(page 1 of 2)

Spouse name (if wife, give maiden name) _____

Lived in present community since _____

Date/place married _____

Occupation(s)_____

_____

_____

Employer(s)_____

_____

_____

Number of years employed _____

City & state where employed _____

Organizational memberships (if you want to list them) _____

_____

_____

_____

_____

_____

Church information _____

_____

_____

_____

(page 2 of 2)

Decision Making/ Treating Options

Decision Making

This section is the guide to use when you must take over for someone no longer able to manage his or her own decisions, typically because of injury, illness, or mental decline. Through this thorny exercise, people can veer off-course, so take your time. You may need to read through the information more than once to absorb the concepts.

This process may surprise you because it won't match your typical approach to making decisions. The major difference is that you'll go through more steps to evaluate options and reach an answer, because you're not considering just what *you* prefer. Rather, you'll be making decisions for another person. And that's an ethical matter.

So how to do the right thing? You must first train yourself to look through the eyes of the other individual, not your eyes. Try to think: what would I want someone else to consider when making decisions for me? Determine what they would want if they were still able to make the decision; if they were choosing based on THEIR judgment. This procedure is called **substituted judgment**: Deciding in accordance with the incapacitated person's choice, not your preference. Keep in mind, their definition of well-being may differ wildly from yours.

To be a credible advocate, you must first investigate the individual's preferences (past & present). This typically requires time, thought, and research. Questions to ask yourself:

- What has the person verbalized or written regarding what they want?
- What do I know from their past actions?
- What is the opinion of those closest to the person?
- Do they have a "Directive to Physician?"
- Did they complete the documents in the Medical chapter of their Blueprint? If so, you can refer to their forms for answers. These include the following:
  - Medical Planning Worksheet
  - Setting of Priorities
  - Listing of Favorites and Fears
  - Concessions

You are to make decisions in accordance with their preferences unless you are absolutely **certain** that harm will result. Don't take that as carte blanche to rule on what is good for them. Resist that impulse; instead, take care to explore and clarify what harm really means to this individual. Your definition of harm could be very different from theirs. Go back to square one: Decide from their perspective, not yours.

Maximize independence, self-reliance, and retained capability for the incapacitated person whenever possible. Although ultimately the overarching decisions *may* end up coming from you, many other choices can be safely retained by the individual. Always consider the least restrictive living environment. This is frequently a challenge because both functional and mental ability may fluctuate from one day to the next. When unsure, rely on professionals for guidance and options. Never be afraid to gather a team around you to review alternatives. Many of the options and much of the information you are sorting through may be totally new to you. Meanwhile, you may have less time than you'd like for all the work needed to do the right thing.

As you proceed, you're also obligated to protect the patient's civil rights and liberties (confidentiality, due process, etc.):

- Everyone has the right to expect that their personal information will remain confidential. This is the law (HIPAA) and an ethical code you should honor. Use caution in casual conversation to avoid revealing what is private. One person might be sensitive about every area of their life while others are fine with their most intimate details being an open book. Since most of us do not know individual preferences about personal matters, a default position of confidentiality is prudent, courteous, and ethical.

- All individuals retain the right to self-determination until adjudicated as incapacitated in court. When there is a question of mental capacity, the determination is made by a physician. After a determination of incapacity, the pre-existing Power of Attorney documents are utilized as the foundation for the named party to assume responsibility. **No Power of Attorney or legal documents can be executed after it is apparent the person has lost capacity.** If Power of Attorney documents are executed when a person is clearly incapacitated, the documents will be judged invalid. Should questions of capacity arise when no Power of Attorney documents are in place, then the probate court can step in to investigate and determine whether guardianship is needed. If guardianship is deemed appropriate, a physician is still required to determine capacity. Even if incapacity is affirmed, the steps to making ethical decisions remain the same as outlined. First consider what the individual would do if he or she were making the decision.

- Avoid conflict of interest. The responsible party's financial or personal benefit should never affect their choices; in fact, even the appearance of conflict of interest could undermine the validity and holding-power of decisions. When there is financial gain or a conflict of interest, the decision maker must be changed to an unbiased person.

- Recognize that others may scrutinize, criticize, and challenge your decisions. A crisis may force you to decide quickly without sufficient information. Ethical decision making steps are not necessarily intuitive. Heightened emotion and fear frequently come into play. Not understanding options can be a huge deterrent to moving forward. Seeking independent opinions from experienced professionals can provide the needed support.

Treatment Options

Treatment choices are made either by the affected individual or by another person using substituted judgment, making decisions according to an incapacitated person's preferences. Treatments are based on the individual's wishes, available resources, and geography.

Wishes of the Individual Regarding Medical Care

Refer back to "Decision Making" as a foundation. Keep this in mind as you consider some basic questions. Did the individual want aggressive care? Did they want life to be preserved in all circumstances? Did they want only comfort care and no invasive medical intervention when dealing with a terminal or irreversible condition? Most people fall into a grey area, not at the extreme edges. Even though a medical intervention is available or offered, you must still consider the individual's wishes before opting to proceed. Far too often, medical interventions are presented as the *right* alternative. We meekly accept the treatment option because it comes from a knowledgeable healthcare professional. Don't get caught in that trap. For every proposed intervention, your confident answer can be "yes," "no," or "I need more information." Stop and think, what would the individual choose? If you are the responsible party, then you are also the official advocate. You have a right and an obligation to slow down the process if necessary. Your position comes with great power and abundant responsibility. Use it wisely.

Hospice

Informed decisions require clarity about what hospice really means. Certain common misconceptions delay hospice involvement. The most overwhelming fallacy is the belief that when hospice starts, medical care stops. This is totally false. What hospice does mean is that patient care focuses on quality of life and comfort rather than aggressive treatments. Frequently this is exactly what elderly people want, to remain in their home and avoid aggressive hospital treatment. Once enrolled in hospice, the individual receives care where he or she resides. This can be in their home, assisted living, dementia facility, or a nursing home. Medicare covers a hundred percent of hospice cost, covering home visits, some disposable supplies, and some medications.

There is never a cost or a downside to getting a hospice assessment. Although admission to hospice is designed for patients with a life expectancy of six months or less, many patients remain on hospice service for a much longer period of time; I've seen it last for years. Other patients actually improve to the point that they *graduate* from hospice care. Graduation comes when the improvement is significant. In those circumstances, the patient can end hospice services and resume traditional medical care.

Another mistaken belief about hospice is that a hospice caregiver will be at the patient's bedside twenty-four hours a day. Again, this is false. Hospice provides *visits* to monitor care and make needed changes in the treatment plan. For patients who require more care than an intermittent visit, the individual on hospice must receive the continuous care by other means. Options for care include facility care, family, long-term care insurance, or privately paid caregivers.

While on hospice, patients do not proceed to aggressive hospital care. All medical treatment is delivered in their home, where life is expected to end naturally. When that time comes, no fire department, EMS, or police arrive to investigate the cause of death. All parties know it is expected. By contrast, for non-hospice patients, all of these entities may descend on the home to complete mandatory investigations. The cause of death must be determined and this can be done only by asking many painful questions. Believe me, you do not want a homicide investigator on the scene when you are dealing with the initial stage of grieving. I've been through this scenario more times than I would like to admit as a result of unexpected deaths or families being resistant to hospice care. Be sure you consider hospice as the gentle alternative to extreme measures.

Financial Resources

Financial resources must be considered. When Stage I documentation has been completed, then knowledge of available resources will be clear. With Stage II in process, some information may be available but not all. If you enter into Stage III with nothing completed, then you are initially making decisions in the dark. It can be costly to age and receive care. The cost can be covered by:

- Medicare—covers medical care and episodic intermittent care in the home. Also covers skilled nursing care following a medical event for a limited period of time. This does not cover hourly care in the home, assisted-living facilities, dementia facilities, or long-term nursing home.

- Medicaid—covers longer-term care for individuals meeting the financial threshold as indigent. Patients cannot simply give their money to another person (usually family) so that they will qualify as "poor" to reap government benefits. However, when a spouse requires long-term nursing home care, financial safeguards can accommodate the other spouse living in the community. Consulting with a knowledgeable Medicaid elder-law attorney is the only way to determine how to become eligible for Medicaid and preserve resources.

- Private Insurance—covers when the individual has medical insurance that is available through a private policy or employer. Generally, it covers medical care similar to Medicare.

- Long-Term Care Insurance—coverage depends on the policy. Typically provides payment for non-medical custodial care, hourly care in the home, assisted living, Alzheimer's facility care, and long-term care in a nursing home.

- Private-Pay—can be expensive and deplete funds quickly. This is a good option when the elderly person has adequate resources to cover the cost of care. However, it is not reasonable to expect family to cover the high cost of private care for an extended period of time. With inadequate resources, the family should contact an elder-law attorney who specializes in Medicaid eligibility.

Human Resources

Regardless of individual wishes and financial resources, there is a need for a responsible party to manage the logistics of care. This can become anything from a part-time to a full-time job. Some questions to consider:

- Who will take the lead? Even if multiple people will share the workload, one individual must coordinate the plan to avoid chaos.

- Who has the available time?

- Who lives near enough to take care of the logistics?

- Who has the relationship with the aging individual to best handle the situation?

- Whose temperament is best to deal with the emotional ups and downs?

- Is this individual without human resources (no family or friends able to take on the role of the responsible party)?

- Does a local Care Manager need to be retained to handle the day-to-day management?

Geographic Implications

- Proximity is a high priority when it comes to the responsible party and facility placement. Seeing your loved one on a frequent basis is more important than the loveliest facility. Family involvement leads to improved care, merely because oversight is present. A shorter distance to drive decreases some of the wear and tear on the responsible party.

- Living in the same town makes a tremendous difference. Understandably, the elderly person has a strong wish to remain in his or her home city. Often, responsible parties have jobs to maintain and families to care for. Support systems may be spread out over a number of distant locations. However, to provide adequate support for an aging individual, a responsible party must be available in the same town. As painful as it is initially, this often requires the elderly person to relocate to where their strongest family support person lives. If this is not possible, then a local Care Manager should be retained to oversee the care and be available as needed.

CHAPTER 13

Care & Placement Options

Recovery and Where to Live for the Long Term

For most of us, aging will force a transition from independence to some form of assistance. In the process, personal autonomy diminishes. Letting go of control is never easy. Too often this challenge is accompanied by crisis, emotional distress, and uninformed decision making.

Review the completed chapters in the *Blueprint to Age Your Way*. Read and think seriously about what would best meet the needs of the individual you are helping (and that may be you). What are their fears and favorites, their priorities, medical wishes?

There are two types of care to draw upon when looking at facilities:

* Acute recovery medical care—paid by insurance while recovering from a short-term episode of illness.

* Long-term care—After recovery, when medical intervention is no longer indicated. That is the time to consider long-term care options.

Acute Recovery Medical Care

To achieve optimum health, an ill or injured patient should exhaust all treatment options to resolve their condition before embarking on permanent long-term care. During recovery from an acute illness, the goal is to achieve the maximum level of wellness, which is unique to each person. Only after the individual has achieved their maximum wellness can appropriate long-term decisions be made. Medicare and other insurance plans will pay for a great deal of the costlier, shorter-term treatment, which is considered *medical care*.

Long-Term Care / Non-Medical Care

After the maximum level of wellness becomes apparent, then permanent-care criteria should become evident. This second level of care is considered custodial or *non-medical care*. Remember, the elderly will typically minimize safety concerns to remain in control and independent. Often the decision requires compromise. It's important to understand that progress can still be made while at the long-term level of care—the primary difference is that acute medical intervention is no longer required. Rather, the gains are occurring as a result of time and the normal healing process.

Placement Alternatives

If the decision is to move into a facility, then start with those facilities geographically nearest to you. Stop by the ones you're evaluating and simply walk in as though visiting someone. Observe the residents to see if they are clean, content, and interacting with attentive staff. Talk with residents and family members to determine their level of satisfaction. You can later take an arranged tour that covers all the amenities. Remember, the beautiful chandelier and artwork will not care for your loved one, only the care staff will. Scrutinize the care being delivered.

The two charts below are to help you better compare the different alternatives for *acute medical care* that is typically covered by insurance and *long-term or non-medical care*. Many people are surprised by the difference so study the charts carefully.

PLACEMENT ALTERNATIVES / LEVEL OF CARE AND PAYMENT OPTIONS

Utilize all medical care in **acute stage** of illness to achieve maximum wellness first.
Then move on to consider long-term placement options.

Location of Care	Average Stay	Type of Care / Information	Payment
Hospital (acute)	2–5 days	Short-term episode of illness.	Medicare, Medicaid, Insurance
Rehab Hospital (acute)	2 weeks	Must tolerate three hours per day of therapy (physical, occupational, speech).	Medicare, Medicaid, Insurance
Long-Term Acute Hospital Care (LTAC)	3–4 weeks	Too ill for nursing home. Too weak for rehab. Qualify for long-term hospital stay.	Medicare, Insurance, Medicaid
Skilled Nursing Facility (SNF)	3–5 weeks (max 100 days)	Skilled care needed (therapy or nursing) as long as medically necessary and making progress up to a hundred days.	Medicare, Insurance. Need three-day inpatient hospital stay to qualify.
Home Health Care (skilled)	Usually 4–8 weeks	Intermittent therapy or nursing if doctor's orders stipulate skilled care, for homebound patient.	Medicare, Insurance, Medicaid to a limited degree.

Once Medicare quits paying—**Long-Term Care** Non-Medical Options for Long Term

Location	Type of Care / How to Qualify	Payment
Nursing home (long-term care)	Must meet medical-necessity threshold to qualify for Medicaid & LTC insurance: need help with two ADLs (activities of daily living) or severe cognitive impairment. Should be medically stable.	Private pay, LTC (long-term care) insurance, Medicaid with financial qualification. VA (veteran's) pension.
Assisted living (residential)	Able to stay alone part-time. Help with care, meals, and medications as needed.	Private pay. LTC Ins. Few Medicaid beds. VA pension.
Dementia facility (long-term care)	Care needed for cognitive reasons. Locked facility required because some patients wander off or have challenging behaviors.	Private pay. LTC Ins. Few Medicaid beds. VA pension.
Personal care (Residential) home	Private home. Unlicensed caregiver available twenty-four hours a day.	Private pay. Very few Medicaid beds.
Hospice	Life expectancy six months or less. Intermittent visits in the home or a facility.	Medicare. Medicaid. Insurance.
Hourly Non-Medical Care at Home	Hourly care can cover a few hours up to twenty-four hours a day.	Private pay. LTC Ins. Medicaid if qualify. VA pension.
Family Care at Home	Caution: family should not try to do it all for the long-term. Have respite coverage for time away.	FMLA (Family Medical Leave Act) to hold job and care by family.

NON-MEDICAL OPTIONS FOR LONG-TERM CARE PLACEMENT

The following grids compare nine primary options available today. In general, the lists flow progressively according to patient status, from independent at first to finally incapacitated and totally dependent. Patients' needs are not static: What seems appropriate today may be completely off-base a year from now. Many people transition from one level of care to the next over time, while some enter a facility needing a higher level of care and never move again.

Consider what would be the best choice for you or the person you are helping.
Document the choices at the end of the grids below.

1. LIVING INDEPENDENTLY IN THE HOME	
When appropriate	Mentally sharp, able to manage personal care, safe from exploitation.
Financial cost	Typical home-maintenance costs.
Payment sources	Private-pay for typical home costs.
Human resources (family, agent)	May need someone to check status or be available for emergencies.
Personal care	Self-manage all activities of daily living (ADLs) such as bathing, dressing, continence, eating, toileting, and transferring.
Safety (physical and financial)	Able to phone for help or push button on a wearable emergency alert if at risk of falls. Aware of solicitation and scamming. Will not provide personal identifying information or purchase non-legitimate services.
Medications	Take independently. Someone else may need to set up med boxes.
Medical care	Go to appointments independently or accompanied by someone else, or have home visiting doctor.
Nutrition	Maintain own meals. Drink adequate fluids. Can fix simple dishes. Meals on Wheels or other home-delivered food also can be arranged.
Transportation	Drive or can utilize other means of transport for groceries and errands.
Add-on services	Housekeeping. Lawn. Anything else needed for the home. Emergency alert system for falls or emergencies.
Medicare-provided services	Intermittent no-cost Medicare visits after episode of illness, with doctor's order, need for some form of skilled service, and if patient is homebound (nursing, therapy, bath aide). Hospice visits for end-of-life care.
Special considerations	Home must be free of fall risks, any stairs safely manageable, bathroom to have grab bars and other safety measures in place.
Clues it's no longer working	Patient is no longer clean, wearing the same clothes every day, losing weight, inadequate food in the home, house dirty, falls, exploitation.

2. LIVING AT HOME WITH CARE ASSISTANCE	
When appropriate	When the home can be made physically safe and trusted caregivers are able to provide needed assistance.
Financial cost	Varies per geographic area. Can typically start at a few hundred dollars a week when care needs are small and intermittent. Dramatically higher cost when twenty-four-hour care required; can be as high as twenty thousand dollars a month in some parts of the country. If patient sleeps well at night, a *live-in* caregiver can be used who sleeps at night also and is paid a flat daily rate. This can reduce cost by a third.
Payment sources for caregivers	Private pay. Long-term care insurance. Medicaid for low income (in some states & some circumstances). VA pension and/or "extended care services" for some veterans and their widow(er)s.
Human resources (family, agent)	Most patients need someone to oversee care—a third party to assure no exploitation by caregivers (sad but true) or others.
Personal care	Caregiver can manage any or all activities of daily living (bathing, dressing, continence, eating, toileting, transferring).
Safety (physical and financial)	Able to phone for help or push button on a wearable emergency-alert if alone for periods of time. Home to be free of fall risks, any stairs to be safely manageable, bathroom to have grab bars and other safety measures in place. Aware of solicitation and scamming. Will not provide personal identifying information or purchase non-legitimate services. Checkbooks, credit cards, and valuables made safe or removed from the home.
Medications	Can be independent or with caregiver assistance.
Medical care	Independently go to appointments, have someone else take, or have home visiting doctor. Search out caregiver who can drive to appointments.
Nutrition	Meals on Wheels or home-delivered foods can continue. Caregiver can grocery-shop and prepare meals.
Transportation	Search out caregiver who can grocery-shop and take on errands/outings.
Add-on services	Housekeeping. Lawn. Emergency alert system. Caregiver.
Medicare-paid services	Intermittent no-cost Medicare visits at no cost after episode of illness, with doctor's order, need for some form of skilled service, and if patient is homebound (nursing, therapy, bath aide). Hospice visits for end-of-life care.
Special considerations	Third party will need to oversee caregivers and monitor finances. Watch that patient is not incrementally paying for more caregiver expenses as dependence grows and patient becomes involved in the caregiver's personal saga. Monitoring the checking account(s) and credit card(s) online with patient's permission may be advisable.
Clues it's no longer working	Depleting financial resources. Patient resisting caregiver help. Denying or refusing need for care. Poor hygiene. Losing weight. Falls. Exploitation.

3. LIVING AT FAMILY MEMBER'S HOME	
When appropriate	When the home can be made physically safe and family is willing to be "on call" twenty-four hours a day, seven days a week. In most situations, this should be for a limited period of time only.
Financial cost	Possible renovation costs to make house appropriate, safe for an elderly or disabled individual. If family is working, caregiver cost may be a part of the financial formula—cost varies with hours of care needed.
Payment sources for caregivers	Private-pay. Long-term care insurance. Medicaid for low-income (in some states & some circumstances). VA pension and/or "extended-care services" for some veterans and their widow(er)s.
Human resources (family, agent)	Human cost is huge as the household changes dramatically. Before proceeding, family should agree in writing on expectations and what would constitute a need to end care in the home. Any family member in the home should have the right to terminate the situation.
Personal care	Can be managed independently or with assistance from family or paid caregiver.
Safety (physical and financial)	Able to phone for help or push button on a wearable emergency-alert if alone for periods of time. Before move-in, fix fall risks, make sure any stairs are safely manageable, install safety measures such as grab bars in bathroom. Be aware of solicitation and scamming when left alone.
Medications	Can be independent or with family or caregiver assistance.
Medical care	Family or caregiver take to appointments, or have home-visiting doctor. Search out caregiver who can drive to appointments.
Nutrition	Meals on Wheels or home-delivered foods can continue in some situations. Family typically takes over meal responsibility.
Transportation	Family or caregiver.
Add-on services by others	Recommend against this emotionally taxing option UNLESS some caregiver hours can be arranged (or patient safe to stay alone for periods of time). Emergency-alert system if alone in the home for periods of time.
Medicare-paid services	Intermittent no-cost Medicare visits after episode of illness, with doctor's order, need for some form of skilled service, and if patient is homebound (nursing, therapy, bath aide). Hospice visits for end-of-life care.
Special considerations	In cases of dementia, observe for tendency to leave the house in an attempt to "go home." If at risk of wandering off, identifying jewelry should be worn at all times for safe return to residence.
Clues it's no longer working	Family fracturing. Depleting resources (financial or emotional). Patient becoming agitated/upset with host family.

4. INDEPENDENT RETIREMENT COMMUNITY / SENIOR APARTMENT LIVING	
When appropriate	Mentally sharp, able to manage personal care, safe from exploitation. Good option when home is no longer physically safe. Apartments are accessible for wheelchairs/walkers + enable socialization.
Financial cost	Vary depending on amenities and geographic area. Some are government-sponsored "low-income housing" with income-based sliding scale rates.
Payment sources	Private-pay. Government-sponsored programs (typically managed by a local housing authority) can offset some cost.
Human resources (family / agent)	Some human-resource support needed as most of these communities provide no additional services beyond a safe layout and socialization.
Personal care	None provided by the community. Must be able to manage independently or engage privately hired help.
Safety (physical and financial)	Apartments provide basic physical safety as they are purpose-built for seniors. Many have emergency-call cord. May also need a wearable emergency-call system if susceptible to falls. Monitor for this.
Medications	Must be independent. Community typically provides no assistance.
Medical care	Independently go to appointments, have someone else take, or have home visiting doctor.
Nutrition	Able to fix simple meals. Meals on Wheels or other home-delivered food can be arranged. Some communities provide meals.
Transportation	Resident drives or can engage other transport for groceries and errands.
Add-on services	Housekeeping. Emergency alert system.
Medicare-paid services	Intermittent no-cost Medicare visits after episode of illness, with doctor's order, need for some form of skilled service, and if patient is homebound (nursing, therapy, bath aide). Hospice visits for end-of-life care.
Special considerations	When moving in to an independent community, realize this is not a final move. Relocation will be necessary when need for support increases. Be prepared for another move or to hire caregivers.
Clues it's no longer working	Patient is no longer clean, wears the same clothes repeatedly, loses weight, lacks adequate food in the home, house dirty, falls, exploitation.

	5. CONTINUING-CARE RETIREMENT COMMUNITY (CCRC) = LIFE-CARE COMMUNITY Provides the option to live in one campus of care for your lifetime. You must be independent at time of entering community. Pay large entrance fee plus monthly fee.
When appropriate	With most communities, you can enter only when functioning independently. As your needs change and health declines, you can move to assisted living, dementia care, or skilled nursing care on the same campus.
Financial cost	Significant entry fee, anywhere from a hundred thousand to a million dollars at outset if buying life-care. Depending on the contract, most of the entrance fee may be reimbursed to heirs at death. Expect additional monthly fees ($3000–$5000 per month), which may grow with care needs. Monthly fees for advanced care are lower than comparable community rates as entrance fees serve to offset costs.
Payment sources	All private-pay. LTC Insurance can begin reimbursing some monthly cost when personal care is needed. VA benefits can also cover some care costs.
Human resources (family, agent)	Intermittent, unannounced visits are recommended to monitor care. Remain available for emergencies.
Personal care	Care follows the same structure as the varying levels of care already discussed (independent, assisted-living, dementia, skilled-nursing).
Safety (physical and financial)	All the risks associated with living alone are present during the independent years. However, staff is available to respond to emergencies. Exploitation from the outside is a risk that needs to be monitored.
Medications	Self when independent. Staff-administered at higher levels of care.
Medical care	Nurse is on-campus for emergencies but these communities are large and an expected wait time for response should be understood. Independent residents can go to their community doctor for routine care or have visiting doctor come to the facility. Doctors make routine rounds at higher levels of care.
Nutrition	Facility provides meals at all levels of care.
Transportation	Transport available for doctor visits. Family should meet for all doctor visits.
Add-on services	Cost of services will increase as needs change. Privately paid caregivers can be added at any time.
Medicare-paid services	After a qualifying hospital stay, the skilled-nursing unit should bill Medicare for the period of time the patient qualifies for a rehab stay. Medicare home-health services are available in the independent setting.
Special considerations	Modified & Fee-for-Service contracts exist also but these are not truly life-care contracts. Be sure you know what you're purchasing. Financial solvency of owner/developers is unregulated, exposing deposits to forfeiture by developer's creditors in the event of bankruptcy. Do your research in advance.
Clues it's no longer working	This option should last a lifetime. However, it requires major financial commitment. So investigate accordingly. Check how the community is meeting needs of residents in declining health. Ask others if they are happy there.

6. ASSISTED-LIVING COMMUNITY	
Patients have their own apartments plus twenty-four-hour attendant care available.	
When appropriate	Mentally sharp or early stage of memory loss. Able to manage most of personal care. Independent toileting. Aware of needs, knows when to ask for help.
Financial cost	Cost varies based on facility, apartment size and services. Current US average for a room is $3600 monthly. Many are cost-structured like a cafeteria plan; added services cost more for each. At outset, confirm starting rate and obtain clear estimate of maximum cost with all services (for budgeting).
Payment sources	Private-pay. Long-term care insurance (LTC) will usually pay if you are receiving personal-care assistance. VA for some veterans and their spouses.
Human resources (family, agent)	In a well-run facility, family involvement only needed for emergencies. However, it is always advisable to make intermittent visits to monitor services and patient status.
Personal care	Varying levels of personal care available. The patient must be able to wait their turn for care, so this type of facility is best-suited for patients who can toilet independently. Additional care services can be purchased for bathing, dressing, night-care, transport to dining room for meals.
Safety (physical and financial)	Emergency-call cords in apartments. May also need to add a wearable emergency-call system for falls. Licensing varies for these facilities. Some communities require patients be able to evacuate independently in an emergency; others can assist emergency evacuation.
Medications	Can be independent or the facility can manage & administer all medications (for additional monthly fee).
Medical care	Independently go to appointments, have someone else take, or have home visiting doctor. Typically, a nurse is on-site during business hours Monday through Friday. Other hours, the facility is staffed with unlicensed care staff.
Nutrition	Meals provided by the facility in a community dining room. If unable to get to meals independently, meal transport is available.
Transportation	Most facilities provide van transportation to doctors and shopping.
Add-on services	Housekeeping provided at no additional fee. Most also do a load of laundry weekly when they change bed linens and wash towels. Additional laundry services usually at an additional fee. Many patients hire personal caregivers in addition to facility staff in an attempt to remain where they are.
Medicare-paid services	Intermittent Medicare visits at no cost after episode of illness, with doctor's order, need for some form of skilled service, and if patient is homebound (nursing, therapy, bath aide). Hospice visits for end-of-life care.
Special considerations	A confused patient who would walk out of the facility and get lost is not appropriate for assisted living except in a "memory care" unit—see "Secured Dementia-Care Facility" below. Depending on the facility's license requirements, the patient may need to move when they can no longer evacuate independently in an emergency. You need to know this in advance. Most facilities allow patients to decline over time and remain in the same apartment with additional support services added on.
Clues it's no longer working	Patient not doing well either due to a poorly-run facility or their needs surpassing what the facility can manage. If patient requires continuous nursing care beyond business hours, then it may be time to move.

7. SECURED DEMENTIA-CARE FACILITY	
Special locked facility that protects patients from wandering out and getting lost or hurt. Staff are trained in dementia care. Most provide safe outdoor walking area for patients. Many standard assisted-living facilities have attached dementia units, a great option.	
When appropriate	When patients walk independently and are at risk to leave. Other patients need this specialized care because of dementia agitation. They require staff who are skilled in redirecting them when upset and staff who can comfort their fears.
Financial cost	Varies greatly based on geography. Average cost is about $5000 monthly. Considerably higher than assisted living but the cost is more stable over time as there are less add-on costs as patients require more care).
Payment sources	Private pay. Rarely, Medicaid. Long-term care insurance. VA pension for some veterans and their spouses.
Human resources (family, agent)	Intermittent visits to monitor care/patient status. Otherwise, as needed for emergencies.
Personal care	All personal care delivered as needed.
Safety (physical and financial)	These are some of the safest facilities in terms of physical well-being. As with any facility, to avoid theft risk, patient shouldn't bring money or valuables.
Medications	Administered by staff.
Medical care	Most have a doctor group conduct on-site visits. To leave for doctor visits or to see a specialist would be the responsibility of family. Most have a licensed nurse on duty during business hours and on-call after hours.
Nutrition	Facility provides meals.
Transportation	Family's responsibility.
Add-on services	No added fees unless an extra charge for adult diapers, nutritional supplements.
Medicare-paid services	Intermittent Medicare visits at no cost after episode of illness, with doctor's order, need for some form of skilled service, and if patient is homebound (nursing, therapy, bath aide). Hospice visits for end-of-life care.
Special considerations	Understand the environment and don't send your loved one there with items of value. Patients often go into rooms of others and take out what they want. There is a fair amount of "sharing" personal belongings. Find out from the start if your loved one can remain for the rest of their life. Most will allow this, facilitating hospice services toward the end of life.
Clues it's no longer working	At the start it will feel as though it's not working. Everyone experiences this. The vast majority of patients don't understand or acknowledge their need for placement. They simply know they're upset and not home. Read the chapter on dementia in the *Age Your Way* story book to better understand. Allow three to six months before considering relocation. Once the patient's difficult behavior or wander-risk abates, they can be moved if needed. However, change is especially disrupting for dementia patients, so move only with great caution and only for a very good reason.

8. RESIDENTIAL CARE HOMES = BOARD & CARE HOMES = PERSONAL-CARE HOMES (PCH)	
These are private homes in residential neighborhoods, staffed with unlicensed caregivers. May or may not be licensed depending on the state and number of patients who live in the home. Some unlicensed facilities are operating illegally but are tolerated for lack of alternatives. Some of the best & worst care is in PCHs. Scrupulous reference checks are imperative.	
When appropriate	With the right ownership and management, most patients can live safely in a care home for the long term. The exceptions are patients inclined to wander off and get lost or those with a high level of agitation as they can easily upset other resident in the house. Additionally, patients who require continuous nursing care aren't appropriate.
Financial cost	Varies greatly based on geography and size. Average cost is about $3000 monthly. Once needs are assessed and rate determined, the cost of monthly care remains more constant than assisted living (fewer add-on costs).
Payment sources	Private pay. In rare circumstances, Medicaid may pay. Long-term care insurance would be on a case-by-case basis.
Human resources (family, agent)	Recommend family oversight with unannounced visits. Since these are smaller homes with less governance, more checking is prudent. Care can vary significantly based on the caregiver on duty. Observe frequently and closely until a comfort level is achieved.
Personal care	Make sure to find out if there are limits on personal care. Most do everything.
Safety (physical and financial)	As long as the environment is free of fall risks and bathrooms accessible, safety is not generally a concern. Smaller homes are not required to have sprinkler systems installed for fire. No money or valuables should go with the patient.
Medications	Administered by staff.
Medical care	Most have a doctor group for home visits. To leave for doctor visits or to see a specialist would be the responsibility of family. Any nursing needs are done by intermittent Medicare home visits. A few PCHs have nurse-owners.
Nutrition	Facility provides meals.
Transportation	Family's responsibility.
Add-on services	No additional fees unless they charge extra for adult diapers or supplements.
Medicare-paid services	Intermittent Medicare visits at no cost after episode of illness, with doctor's order, need for some form of skilled service, and if patient is homebound (nursing, therapy, bath aide). Hospice visits for end-of-life care.
Special considerations	Most are quiet environments with minimum stimulation, appealing to some patients who enjoy quiet. This can be a wonderful long-term solution as remaining until the end of life is the norm. Just don't forget to monitor care.
Clues it's no longer working	Patient not doing well either due to a poorly run facility or their needs surpassing what the facility can manage. Typically raises a decision point: additional medical care versus hospice. If choosing more medical care, transfer to a nursing facility. Hospice care can be delivered in the home without a move.

9. NURSING FACILITY (NF) — LONG-TERM NURSING CARE	
Can be for short-term rehabilitation or long-term custodial care. Be prepared as they are homes to patients with varying levels of physical and mental impairments.	
When appropriate	After an inpatient hospital stay, patients who meet requirements can be admitted under Medicare payment for rehabilitation. Medicare pays for a limited time. Then, the patient can leave or may be able to remain long term. With a Medicare stay, think about discharge plans from the start as Medicare can end quickly. An admission that is not following a hospitalization and simply based on a growing need for more care can be less complicated. Dementia patients without highly agitated behaviors or wander-risk are also appropriate for nursing facility care.
Financial cost	See Medicare-paid services below. Average monthly cost for long-term nursing facility care is just under $7000 per month nationally. Medicare and Medicaid pay for a semi-private room, so your loved one may have a roommate unless you privately pay for a private room.
Payment sources	Medicare and supplement for the initial rehab period after a qualifying hospitalization. Private-pay. LTC Insurance. Medicaid if qualify financially and medically. VA pension for some veterans and their spouses.
Human resources (family, agent)	Need to stay closely engaged during a Medicare stay as plans are needed for what comes next. From the start, find out if staying long-term is an option or not. Additional work may be required for next steps. For long-term cases, unannounced visits at varying times of the day and night are best.
Personal care	All personal care delivered as needed.
Safety (physical and financial)	One of the biggest risks is confusion after hospitalization which can lead to falls. No money or valuables should go to the facility with the patient.
Medications	Administered by staff.
Medical care	Nurses on site 24 hours a day. Doctors visit. Van transport may be available for community doctor visits. Family must meet at the appointment.
Nutrition	Meals provided by the facility.
Transportation	Most have transport available for doctor visits.
Add-on services	No additional fees during Medicare days. After that, expect a daily fee, cost of medications, disposable supplies (adult diapers, wipes, etc.).
Medicare-paid services	Medicare stay: entire cost paid by Medicare the first 20 days. After that there is a daily copay *for as many days that you qualify, up to a total of 100 days, under Medicare regulations (skilled care being medically beneficial).* Few patients meet medical criteria for the full 100 days.
Special considerations	Be prepared from the start with a plan in place to where you go next. If funds are limited and you will be trying to qualify your family member for a long-term Medicaid-paid bed, then it is best to begin the rehab stay in a facility where a Medicaid bed is an option. You may need a case manager and/or Medicaid Elder Law Attorney to assist with this.
Clues it's no longer working	Sometimes, elderly patients admitted to skilled-nursing-facility rehab are unwilling or unable to make the effort for rehab progress. This will shorten the time Medicare will reimburse for the stay. Stay in close touch with the staff (usually the social worker) to have a sense when Medicare days will end. The silver lining of these stays is that it can give you an inside look at a nursing facility to determine if this might be a good option long-term for your loved one.

PERSONAL CHOICES FOR LONG-TERM CARE OPTIONS

List, in order of priority (1, 2, 3) what choices you would make.

So You Are Finished! Now What?

- Meet with the responsible party or family to **share the life guide,** a precious compilation of information to benefit both the individual and family. As noted earlier, **annual meetings** between the individual and designated parties enable updates so the Blueprint stays useful by reflecting changing situations. In addition, face-to-face meetings can enhance relationships and extend mutual understanding.

- Complete the *Distribution Document.* This form follows the *Table of Contents* for handy access to **track who has copies of what part of the plan.**

- Keep the Blueprint where it will be **safe** yet easy to find in a time of need. This may be tricky. You don't want just anyone to lay hands on this trove of financial and personal data. No one should be able to see and use it apart from those you designate. Lock away the entire Blueprint and associated files — but **make sure your inner circle has access,** day or night, in case of emergency. It's this access that will allow quick decisions in accordance with your stated wishes.

- Pass on the *passion for planning!* Who else needs to plan? It's time to brag about what you've accomplished and spread the word to others. After all, a completed Blueprint is the best option to *Age Your Way.*

For more information and to order additonal copies, visit
www.CareFor.com

Gratitude

As a novice writer in my sixties, I have a long list of people to thank for helping this passion become a reality. It's hard to know where to begin.

First, my patients: You have touched my soul in a manner that lingers, long after the physical touch has ended. The lasting feelings, joys, and sorrows are forever etched in my heart. You have all been such a gift. Throughout the years, you have welcomed me into your lives in a way that I cherish and respect. In lockstep with my patients have been their loving families and caregivers who were the difference makers. I marvel at all you willingly give to enrich the lives of our patients. Thank you for allowing me in. For without you, there would be no stories to tell, no passion to plan.

For the professionals I have had the honor to work with, I thank you: The judges, attorneys, trust officers, physicians, nurses, social workers, and countless other experts. Because of you, I've grown personally and professionally. Your example and gentle push taught me how to embrace problems with enthusiasm.

For the family of Nurses Case Management, there are too many to thank. To my partners, Jack and Ben, the epitome of ethical business leaders, you are the greatest treasure my company received. To Catherine and Gary, your willingness to take over the daily reins allowed the company to grow and soar. To the nursing and operations staff, I am in awe of all you accomplish as a cohesive team that continues to always put the patients first.

To those of you who did the hand-holding necessary to take me through the crash course of writing and publishing, I'm in awe of you. Janica, Dennis, Marti, Sylvia, Tami, and Monica: both your patience and guidance are beyond description. Starting out with the A-Team the first time out was a stroke of luck and true blessing.

To my family, you are the world to me. Our three children have surpassed our greatest hopes and dreams, much of which is due to the remarkable spouses they chose. It is a gift to love and admire the six of you. I marvel at your ability to juggle all you do while demonstrating grace under pressure. Our eight grandchildren are the ultimate reward, the promise of a glorious future.

And to my Hank, my heartbeat, my soulmate, the best husband and father in the world, words are inadequate to express my feelings. Sharing life with you has been the best thing that ever happened. Partnering with you in the publishing was icing on the cake. Together we stumbled through the process, knowing little, laughing much, and welcoming the journey of learning what to do next. The humor and delight you brought into our lives many years ago continues to this very day. You are my most precious goofball.

About the Author

DEBBIE PEARSON, RN has a mountain of experience in helping patients in chaos. Her forty-year career began as a hospital nurse, then a home health care nurse, a case manager, and court appointed guardian. She founded Nurses Case Management in 2000 to advocate for people who could no longer care for themselves due to age, injury or illness.

Her credentials include a Bachelor of Science in Nursing, Nationally Certified Case Manager, Aging Life Care Professional, and Texas Certified Guardian. Her lifelong commitment to "patient first" has guided her years of caring and has culminated in the writing of a two-book series: *Age Your Way* and *The Blueprint to Age Your Way*.

Debbie's a motivational speaker on the topic of planning for the aging years ahead. Her real-life stories illuminate the need to move forward in advance of the need, execute your blueprint, and prevent medical mayhem. If you are interested in booking Debbie for a speaking engagement, you can visit www.CareFor.com.

Debbie lives in Austin with her husband, Hank. They have three children and eight grandchildren.

CPSIA information can be obtained
at www.ICGtesting.com
Printed in the USA
LVHW071121150122
708244LV00005B/13